やはり
辞任することにした

いろいろ
考えたが……

And decided to resign.

I've thought it over a great deal ...

私も初芝電産の社長を4期 8年も務めた
ここ5年間の業績不振の責任もとらなければ
ならないだろう

I've been the president of Hatsushiba Electric for 4 terms—8 years. I have to take responsibility for the poor results of the past 5 years.

ひょっとしたら キミのところにも
影響が及ぶかもしれないが……
少し覚悟してくれ

Yes, sir.

This could have an effect on your position as well.

はい

SUNSHINE I

Headquarters of
Hatsushiba Electric

初芝電産本社

Meeting of the
board of directors

取締役会

最後に私から
皆さんにお伝えしたい
ことがあります

以上　来期の
建て直しを念頭に置いて
今期の業務を全うして下さい

And finally, I'd like to make an announcement.

That's it. We'll rest our hopes on a recovery in the coming year.

?

Our profits have been faltering since the collapse of the bubble, and ultimately, in the previous fiscal year, we registered a loss.

初芝電産は
バブル崩壊後
低迷を続けておりましたが
前期はとうとう
赤字決算となりました

SKKTTT

今期　何とか持ち直そうと
努力いたしましたが力及ばず
2期連続で赤字となることが
確実となりました

その責任をとりまして
私はこの度(たび)
代表取締役社長を
辞任いたしたいと思います

> In the year just ending, we made every effort to recover but were unsuccessful. It's now certain that we'll record losses for two consecutive years.

> Accepting full responsibilty for that, I'd like to tender my resignation as president and CEO.

後任の人事に関しては
これから大泉会長と相談して決定いたします
発表は2週間後
もう一度臨時取締役会を開いて
そこでいたします

> Our chairman, Mr. Oizumi, and I will be conferring about my successor. We'll announce our decision in 2 weeks, at another special meeting of the board.

なお　この件に関しては
来年の決算役員会で　マスコミに発表し
その後　2月の株主総会で
決議されますので
それまでは口外せぬよう
各位にお願い申しあげます

以上
閉会！

That's all. Meeting adjourned!

This will be announced to the media at the audit meeting next year and ratified at the meeting of shareholders in February. Please don't disclose this to anyone until that time.

北鎌倉
大泉裕介別邸

Yusuke Oizumi's villa in Kita-Kamakura

9

Show him in.

Mr. Nakazawa is here to see you.

Sir?

With your permission.

業績不振の責任は
この私にあります

はい 勝手を申しますが 私が推進した
コスモス映画買収も ベトナムの半導体工場も
今となっては すべて失敗に終わりました

Responsibility for our poor showing lies with me.

Yes. The acquisition of Cosmos Movies and the semiconductor plant in Vietnam, both of which I pushed forward, have ended in failure.

辞めるんだって？

今 本社から
連絡をもらった

You're quitting?

I just got word from headquarters

ベトナムの半導体工場だって キミが社長になる
ずっと前から 話は進められていた
……特に責任を感じることもあるまい

And the plant in Vietnam—those plans were in motion well before you became the president … You needn't feel any particular responsibility.

何を言ってる
コスモス買収は
私が命令したことだ

Nonsense. I'm the one who insisted we acquire Cosmos.

はい しかし コスモス映画を手放さざるを得なかったのも
私の責任ですし ベトナムの工場の閉鎖も
16メガバイトDRAM（ディーラム）の
将来を予測出来なかった私の責任です

But it's my fault we had to let Cosmos go, and my inability to foresee the lack of demand for 16-megabyte DRAMs led to the closing of the semiconductor plant.

まあな…… これは別に
うちだけじゃなくて ソラーも東立も含めて
業界全体 日本全体が同じ状況なんだけどな……

う——ん……

Well, it's not just us. The entire industry, including Sora and Toritsu—all of Japan, in fact—is in the same boat.

Mmm …

守りの経営をさせれば
彼の方が上です！
ただ年齢が
もう60歳というのが
気になりますが……

そうですね
岡林副社長は実力派です
今まで特に失敗らしい失敗を
したことがないのが特長です
とにかく堅実派ですね

If we're thinking in terms of conservative management, to maintain our position, he's our man. But he's 60, and his age concerns me ...

Yes, sir. Mr. Okabayashi is a capable man, distinctive for having made no missteps to speak of. He's steady and solid.

経営は攻めのタイプなので
不況の時には　難しいかもしれません

万亀君は岡林君より4年若くて
企画力があります　義理人情に厚く
部下から慕われているのは彼の方です

But his management style is more aggressive, which could be a problem in these recessionary times.

Mr. Mangame is 4 years younger and has great planning abilities. He's a loyal and compassionate man, and has the edge in terms of the devotion afforded him by his subordinates.

では……
失礼いたします

よし　明日は
この2人にあって
いろいろ話を聞いてみよう

Very good, sir. I'll leave you, then.

All right. I'll meet with both of them tomorrow and sound them out.

13

はい　島ですが

Shima speaking.

あ！
社長

私だ
中沢だ

Hello, sir!

It's me. Nakazawa.

今　車の中だ
東名高速を
東京(そっち)へ向かっている

I know this is sudden, but do you have time for a drink or two tonight?

I'm calling from my car. We're on the Tomei Expressway, headed for Tokyo.

急な電話で何だが……
今晩　ちょっと
飲む時間はあるか？

14

うん
今後のことだ

I want to
discuss
what's
next for
you.

はい……

Yes,
sir.

Is
there
...

?

何か？

CLUB
BASARA

15

さ　島君！
次行こか!!

Let's move on to the next place, Shima!

やだあ
中沢ちゃんたら
いやらしい～～

カカカカ

Ha, ha, ha!

Mr. Nakazawa! You nasty boy!

はい！

Yes, sir!

いけず　　　　ベー　　　　　　じゃな

You stinker!

Nyah!

See ya.

え～～
もう帰っちゃうの
さっき来たばかりじゃない？

Bye.

You're leaving already? But you just got here!

かしこまりました

新宿のゴールデン街へ
行ってくれないか

...

Yes, sir.

Take us to Golden Lane in Shinjuku.

16

Eiichi Okabayashi,
Vice President

Shosuke Akai,
Managing Director

Isao Narahashi,
Executive Director

しかしまいったな
辞任されてしまうとは…………
先をこされたという感じだ

He sure threw us a curve. To think he'd resign like that … I feel as if Nakazawa got the jump on us.

クーデター不発
というところだな

So the coup d'état has been aborted.

そうですね　来年1月の決算役員会の時に
中沢社長の解任動議を出そうと
準備をすすめていたところなのに……

Yes. Just when we were preparing to propose his removal at the audit meeting in January.

ま　大丈夫でしょう
今の状況からみて
次期社長は岡林副社長がなられるのは
まず　間違いありませんから……

I wouldn't worry. As things stand, Mr. Okabayashi, you're sure to be the one they select.

これで次期社長候補の旗頭に立つという目論見(もくろみ)が
崩れてしまった……辞任という形になると
社長に後任人事権が残ってしまうからなあ
まずいぞ……

So much for our plan to establish myself as the leading candidate for the next presidency … With him resigning he retains the right to select a successor. That's not good …

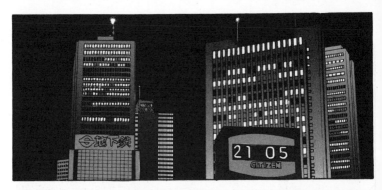

SCREE

Kentaro Mangame,
Vice President.

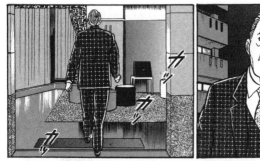

CLACK CLACK
CLACK

副社長
万亀 健太郎

お帰りなさい　あなた

Hello, dear! Welcome back.

節子さんのところへ
戻ってたの？

Were you staying with Setsuko?

どうしたの
ここんとこずっと
来てくれなかったじゃない

It's been so long. Where have you been?

いや　自宅には戻ってない
女房とも1ヵ月近く
顔を合わせてない

No. I haven't been home or seen my wife for almost a month.

とにかく忙しくて
会社の近くのシティホテルで
寝泊まりしているんだ

My! So these are hard times even for Hatsushiba…

I've been so busy I've had to stay at a hotel near the office.

へえ　ハッシバも
今　大変なんだ

中沢社長が
辞めることになった

Nakazawa's resigning as president.

うん 業績不振の
責任をとって……
ということなんだが

あら‼
どうして？

He's taking responsibility for our poor showing.

Goodness! Why?

私が今 忙しいのも
ベトナムに進出した半導体工場を
閉鎖する作業を進めているからだ
DRAM(ディーラム)の不振も
中沢さんの責任になってくるからな

We're closing down the semiconductor plant in Vietnam, which is what's kept me so busy. The slump in DRAM sales is on Nakazawa's shoulders, too.

21

確かこの辺だったな
キミが私を連れて来て
社長に就任することを
説得した店は……

I'm sure it was right around here. The place you took me to when you convinced me to accept the presidency.

あ　チャコですね

Where are we going?

どこへ
行くんですか？

Oh, you mean Chaco.

But that was 8 years ago. I wonder if it's still here ...

でもあれから
8年経ってますから
まだあるかどうか……

CREAK

There it is!

あったよ！

どうぞォ

Have a seat.

いらっしゃい！

Welcome!

あら　お客さん
前に来られて
たんですか

Oh, you've been here before?

へえ
中は少し
変わったな

It's changed a bit inside.

24

ちょうど
この席に座りましたね

We sat in these same seats, too.

うん　8年前に一度
この2人で

The two of us, just once, 8 years ago.

あ　あなたは
お子さんなんだ……
で　お母さんは？

So you're her daughter? And she …?

じゃ
私の母がやっていた時ね

When my mother was here, then.

なるほど
それまで勤めていた
会社を辞めて？

I see. Quitting the job you'd had till then?

うん　5年前に
亡くなってね……
それ以来私が　この店継いでるの

Passed away 5 years ago. I took over after that.

そうですか
いいお店だ

Well, it's a nice place you've got.

いいかげん
向こうの暮らしにも
飽きてたところだったので
お店を継ぐことにしたの

So I decided to come back and carry on the business.

いーえ　私は
若い頃ロンドンに渡って
そこでずーっと
プー太郎していたの

No. I frittered my youth away in London. But I'd grown a bit bored with my life there.

うむ　このままいけば
社長は岡林副社長になるだろう

出向？

Mm-hm. It looks as if Mr. Okabayashi is likely to succeed me.

Transfer?

しかし　岡林グループは私を快くは思っていない
かねてから私に対する不穏な動きが
あったことも知っている……
私を追放する多数派工作を画策している
という情報も耳にはいってきていた

But the Okabayashi faction are no fans of mine. For some time I've been aware of threatening moves they've made against me. I heard they were maneuvering to build a majority in favor of forcing me out.

My sudden resignation was a surprise move to prevent that sort of power struggle from throwing the company into disorder.

私が突然
不意打ちをくわせるように辞任したのも
そういう抗争で
社内がゴタゴタするのを避けるためだった

26

はい……

一掃といっても　私は派閥を
持たないから　私に近いごく少数の
人間を切ってゆくだろう

おそらく岡林は
社長になったら
中沢色を一掃するだろう

Yes, sir …

I say "all my people," but since I don't have a faction, that simply means the few who've been close to me.

If Okabayashi becomes CEO, all my people will probably be swept out.

そうなると
出向先の希望は通らなくなる
役職も格下げになる可能性もある

つまり　このままだとキミは
早期退社を勧められるか
関連会社への出向だ

In which case you'd have no choice as to where you're transferred. And you might be demoted.

In other words, at this rate you'll probably either be asked to leave or be transferred to an affiliate.

それなら私がまだ社長のうちに
キミの希望する関連会社へ好条件で
行ってもらおうかと思うんだ……

That being so, I thought I'd send you to an affiliate that appeals to you, under favorable conditions, while I'm still the president.

はい……私は
出向に関しては　いっこうに構いませんが
希望する会社といっても　想像がつきません

どうだ　しばらく
ハツシバを離れてみんか
気分転換にもなる

Yes, sir … I don't mind being transferred. But I have no idea what sort of company would appeal to me.

What do you think? Going elsewhere might make for a refreshing change.

27

彼女はコスモス映画売却の
あとは　同じロスにある
初芝電産貿易で
働いています

After we sold Cosmos Movies she remained in L.A. working for Hatsushiba Trading.

キミの部下だった
大町君は　今
どこにいるんだ？

Where's your former subordinate Ms. Omachi these days?

ワイン輸入部門にいて
たぶん今
ワインの買い付けで
フランスに行ってると
思いますが……

She's in the wine import division. I think she's in France right now, purchasing wines ...

28

しかし私はワイン
のことは あまり
よく知らないので……

は……

I don't know much about wine.

Yes, but

そりゃいい そこに行け！
不景気風の吹く日本で ワインに関しては
国民の消費マインドが唯一上がっている
注目の業界だ やりがいはあるぞ

ワインか！

That's perfect! Wine is the one product that's been gaining ground among Japanese consumers since the recession hit. It's a field that's attracting a lot of attention. Well worth pursuing.

Wine!

私の力が及ぶかどうか
わかりませんが

はい……
わかりました！

But I'll give it my best shot!

You overestimate me, sir ...

大丈夫だ！末端のことは担当者に
やらせればいい キミは代表権を持った
専務取締役で出向させよう
日本の景気を引きあげる原動力となってくれ‼

That's all right! Leave the particulars to the people in charge of those things. You'll be the representative executive director. Let's transfer you there. You can help lift the Japanese economy out of this slump!

そんなことは
してくれなくても……

あ ハハハ

新しい門出を
お祝いしなくちゃ‼

あら よかった
じゃない‼

No need for that ...

Ah! Ha, ha!

A brand new start! We must celebrate!

My! Isn't that great! ♡

ハハハ
そりゃそうだ

でもこんな狭い店で2人で
大きな声でしゃべるんだもの
聞こえちゃうよね

ごめんなさい
話 聞いちゃって…… あなた達が
そんな偉い人達とは知らなかったわ

Ha, ha! That's true.

But I can't help overhearing when you talk so loudly in a little place like this!

I didn't realize you were such important gentlemen. Forgive me for eavesdropping ...

とっておきの
ワインよ!!

It's
a bottle
I've been
saving.

はい これ私からの
プレゼント!!
お祝いにあげましょう

Here's
a little
something
in honor
of the
occasion!

んー ロンドンで
つきあっていた元カレシが
ワインの仕事をしてたから

Mmph.

know. My
ex-
boyfriend in
London was
in the wine
business.

……失礼だが こんな高価で
貴重なワインが
よくここに置いてあるな……

え?
※ル・パン
じゃないか

Forgive me,
but I wouldn't
expect you to
have such a
valuable wine
here …

* Whoa.
That's
Le Pin!

POP!

SERIES81／おわり

※ル・パン……フランス・ボルドーのポムロル地区の稀少なワイン。
歴史は浅いがロンドンの市場で高い評価を得て、一躍高値になった。一説によると
この'86年のもので14万円程度、年によっては約55万円の値をつけているものもある
（以下、ワインの価格は全て、'98年10月現在のもの）。

SERIES 8

SUNSHINE II

Letter of Appointment
Mr. Kosaku Shima

But under the circumstances ... Well, think of it as being to your advantage.

I never thought I'd be handing you a notice of transfer to another company ...

Thank you, sir.

島 耕作 殿

右の者 本日をもって 初芝電器産業株式会社より出向し
初芝電産貿易株式会社 代表取締役専務として赴任することを命ずる

代表取締役社長 中沢喜一

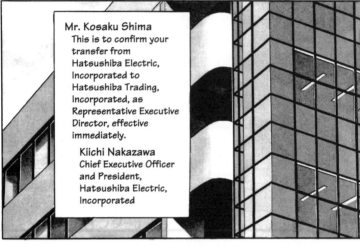

Mr. Kosaku Shima
This is to confirm your
transfer from
Hatsushiba Electric,
Incorporated to
Hatsushiba Trading,
Incorporated, as
Representative Executive
Director, effective
immediately.

Kiichi Nakazawa
Chief Executive Officer
and President,
Hatsushiba Electric,
Incorporated

7F	HONGO ACCOUNTING OFFICE	5F	HATSUSHIBA TRADING, INC.
6F	HATSUSHIBA TRADING, INC.	4F	HATSUSHIBA TRA
		3F	AZABU ESTH

7F　本郷会計事務所

6F　初芝電産貿易K.K.

5F　初芝電産貿易K.K.

4F　初芝電産貿

3F　麻布エスラ

2F　フリマインタ

ZOOOT

SLAM

33

これまでは初芝本社で8年間
総合宣伝部を担当しておりましたが
この度(たび) 初賀(ハツボウ)という "新天地" で
仕事をさせてもらうことになりました

今日から初芝電産貿易(ハツボウ)で
お世話になります島です

For the past 8 years I managed the advertising division at the Hatsushiba headquarters. Now I've been given the opportunity to work with you here. It's new territory for me.

I'm Kosaku Shima. Today is my first day at Hatsushiba Trading.

貿易業務に関しては 全くの新参者です
しばらくの間はいろいろと 皆さんにごめんどうを
おかけすると思いますが 何卒よろしくお願い申し上げます

I'm a complete novice at the trading business, and I'm sure I'll be a bit of a burden to you all at first. I humbly beg your patience and support.

CLAP CLAP CLAP

CLAP CLAP

まあ
かけたまえ

初芝電産貿易
社長　樋口文人

Bunjin Higuchi, president of Hatsushiba Trading

Have a seat.

島君
キミは何年入社だっけ

What year did you enter the company?

失礼します

Thank you, sir.

そうか
僕は39年入社だ
乾電池事業部に配属された

I see. I was hired in 1964. Started out in the dry-cell battery division.

昭和45年入社です
まだ　初代の
吉原初太郎社長の時代でした

In 1970. The founder, Hatsutaro Yoshiwara, was still the president then.

会社法上の別会社ということで
実質は初芝電産の中の
違う部署に来たと思ったらいい

Under corporate law it's a separate company, but in fact it's more like another division of Hatsushiba Electric.

ま　出向といってもな
島君……　この会社は
女子事務員を除いては
半分近くが初芝電産の社員だ

Technically you may have been transferred, but nearly half the people here —excepting the younger female clerks—are employees of HE.

あ
なかなかいいな
今まで自分専用の部屋なんて
持ったことがないから

Chizuru
Takaichi,
secretary

どうですか
専務室のご感想は？

It's great!
I've never had
my own office
before.

秘書
高市千鶴

How do
you like
your office,
Mr.
Shima?

今までの部屋が
ダサかったから

Mm

Hm

嬉しいわ！
私のセンスで
模様がえしたんです

Who
was it
who had
this
office
before?

It was
geeky-
looking
before.

I'm so
glad you
like it! I
oversaw
the
redecora-
ting
myself.

今まで ここに
住んでいた人は
誰だっけ……

Ah ... Well, maybe so ... Heh, heh.

They're pretty loose over at headquarters, aren't they!

What? No one even told you that?

Well, let's call a spade a spade. He was downsized ... Fired.

Mr. Kusumoto, the previous executive director, was in here. He had 5 years to go till retirement, but they got him to retire early because you were coming.

If anybody should be downsized, it was that old coot. All he did was doze in his chair all day.

Don't worry!

I ... I'm sorry to hear that.

Oh?

This secretary won't be easy to deal with ...

初芝電産貿易K.K.は従業員数240名
初芝電産が持株100パーセントの子会社だ
取り扱う輸入品目は欧米の家具
食器　住宅機器関連商品
そして　ワイン　食品など多岐にわたる

Hatsushiba Trading, Inc. employs 240 people. It's an affiliate of Hatsushiba Electric, which owns 100% of its stock. We import a great variety of products including US and European furniture, tableware, and household appliances, as well as wine and foodstuffs.

特に　ワインの輸入量は
ここ5年で3倍に伸びた
ワイン輸入部門は6名いるが
そのうちの1人が大町久美子だ

Wine imports have done particularly well, increasing 300% in the past 5 years. There are six employees in the wine import division, and one of them is Kumiko Omachi.

はい！　専務室

Just a moment, please.

Mr. Shima's office.

少々
お待ち下さい

RINNGGG

あ
すまん

切りかえます

Yes. Thanks.

Shall I put her through?

鳥専務！
フランスの大町社員から
国際電話です

Mr. Shima! Ms. Omachi is calling from France.

KLATCH

嬉しいわ　今日から
私の上司になるのね

I'm so happy to know you're my boss now.

はい　島です

This is Shima.

あ　そうだな
これからもよろしく
お願いします

Ah, right. I look forward to working with you.

今　早朝のブルゴーニュの
ヴォーヌ村の畑の中を
歩いてるの

Walking through vineyards outside the village of Vosne in Burgundy.

今　どこに
いるんだ？

Where are you right now?

39

On my left are the Romanée-Conti vines, already harvested. Beyond them is the Richebourg vineyard. Ahead of me, Romanée-St-Vivant, and on my right I can see La Tâche.

ロマネ・コンティ……世界で最も高い価格で取り引きされるワイン。
畑の広さは1.8ha、平均の生産量はおよそ7千本。'85年で1本約72万円。
他の3つの銘柄も同様に、ブルゴーニュを代表する高価で味・香りともに
秀逸なワイン。　　（講談社刊『世界の名酒事典'99』より）

左手には収穫を終わった*ロマネ・コンティの畑
その奥にはリシュブール
前方にはロマネ・サン・ヴィヴァン
右手にはラ・ターシュの畑が見えるわ

今は世界的に
赤ワインの
ブームだもの

そうね　今言った畑の
ワインは　どの銘柄も
おそろしく高い値段で
取り引きされているわ

ハハハ
そう言われても
ロマネ・コンティくらい
しかわからないな……

There's a worldwide boom for red wine now.

Yes, well, they're all names of terribly expensive wines.

Ha, ha, ha. Romanée-Conti's the only name I recognize …

40

とりあえず現地(こっち)に来て！ 初賢(ハツボー)のワイン部門は
今 我が社の花形なんだから
新専務としては 視察しなきゃいけないと思うわ！

First of all, come have a look for yourself! HT's wine division is the star of the company right now. As the new executive director, you need to see these regions firsthand!

そうだな 私も
おいおい勉強してゆくよ

Right. I'll bone up on all this bit by bit.

KLATCH

わかった……うん
近いうちに そうしよう

OK ... I'll do that sometime soon.

いや 親しいというか
以前 私の下で
働いてたことがあるんだ

FOOF

専務 あの女と
親しいんですか？

Close? I wouldn't say that, but ... We've worked together before.

Are you and that woman close?

変なかんぐりは
よせ！！

高市くん！

道理で なれなれしい
口のききかたを
されてましたこと！

あッ
そう

Stop imagining things!

Takaichi!

No wonder you speak so familiarly to her.

Oh, I see.

41

コピーとりに
行ってきまーす

I have to make some copies.

な——んてね

Very suspicious!

あーら
怒るところが
またまた怪しい

Oh, my, now we're getting angry.

やれやれ
これからが大変だ

Phew! She's going to be a handful.

SLAM

Hatsushiba headquarters

初芝本社

副社長
岡林栄一

Eiichi Okabayashi, vice president

42

もし　キミが社長になるとしたら
これからのハッシバを
どう作りかえてゆくか教えて欲しい

I'd like you to tell us what you'd do to revitalize Hatsushiba if you were the president.

今までの投資が
無駄になることを恐れていては
赤字を減らすことは出来ません

はい　当面すべきことは
赤字部門は
どんどん撤収してゆくことです

We can't cut our losses if we're afraid of writing off prior unwise investments.

Yes, sir. First we must begin eliminating the departments that are operating at a loss.

なるほど
今は
"臥伏の時"と
いうことか

不況の時は臥薪嘗胆(がしんしょうたん)です
傷ついたケモノがケガを治す時は
何日もじっと動かず　ひたすら体を
やすめているそうです

I see. So now's a time for lying low.

During an economic slump, one must bide one's time and persevere. They say that when an animal's wounded, it will remain immobile for days at a time, resting its body in order to heal.

とりあえず
自分の体を治して
世の中の景気が上向いてきた時に
他企業よりゆっくり出て
攻勢をかけていくという
ハッシバ伝統のやり方でいくべきだと思います

私は　これから5年間は
全社一体となって
耐えるべきだと思っています
役員給与はカット
交際費や事務費など
削減出来ることは　積極的にすすめます

Once we've healed our own wounds and the economy begins to recover, we should pursue the time-tested Hatsushiba strategy of emerging more cautiously than other firms before going on the offensive.

I believe that the next 5 years, all of us in the company must tighten our belts and dig in. I strongly urge salary cuts for all executives, and reducing entertainment and office expenses.

はい
岡林副社長のいうことは
正論だと思います

どう思う？

Yes, sir. I think Mr. Okabayashi's argument is sound.

What do you think?

でも
正論だよな……

私も同感です

正論だが　わしは
どうも好かん

It is sound, though.

I feel the same way.

It's sound, but I don't like it.

CHEW CHEW

Nice ball!

グッ
スウィング

SMACK

うわあ
飛んだあ……

あ　ありがとうございます

副社長
万亀健太郎
まんがめけんたろう

Kentaro Mangame, vice president

Woo! Look at it go …

Thank you.

おいおい
ちゃんと仕事してんのか？
心配だなあ

Ah, ha, ha! I'm playing above myself today.

Are you sure you're spending enough time at work?

あ　ハハハ
今日は出来がよすぎます

45

今ベトナムで DRAM (ディーラム) の
工場を閉鎖する作業を進めておりますが
あのまま売却するよりも
売り上げが期待出来る部門の
生産ラインに転換することも
視野に入れております

私は　どちらかと言えば
この時期だからこそ
逆にアグレッシブに
やってみたいと思っています

At the moment I'm involved in closing down the DRAM plant in Vietnam. But rather than simply selling off the facilities, I'm considering the possibility of manufacturing some other product with more promise.

Personally I feel that, precisely because we are in a recession, now's the time to go on the offensive.

46

※ヘッジファンド……空売り・空買いなどの手段を用いて、高い投資効率をねらう、近年拡大中のファンド。

はい　そうです
もちろんリスクは
ともないますが……

Exactly. Of course there are risks involved, but ...

うむ……ということは　ハツシバが先陣をきって
日本の景気をひっぱりあげる
牽引車の役割を果たしたいと……

Hm ... So you'd like Hatsushiba to take a leadership role in lifting the Japanese economy out of the doldrums.

ところで万亀君　キミには
長年つきあっている愛人(オンナ)がいるよな

By the way, Mr. Mangame, I understand you've had a mistress for many years.

なるほど

I see.

今や　写真週刊誌のターゲットは
芸能人やプロ野球選手ばかりじゃない
実業界のトップだって狙われる時代だ

Nowadays the tabloids target business leaders as well as celebrities and baseball players and so on.

はい……
何か？

Yes, sir. And ...?

ましてや　そのターゲットが
世界のハツシバ新社長だったとしたら　どうだろうか……
政財界の醜聞(スキャンダル)のひとつとして
格好のえじきになることも十分考えられる

What if they were to target the new president of a world-class organization like Hatsushiba? One can imagine that a scandal in financial and political circles might be right up their alley.

社長のポストをとるか
女をとるか……
この二者択一を迫られたら
キミはどうする？

そうかもしれません

彼女とは20年来のつきあいです
今更　棄てるわけにはいきません

女をとります

49

うん　驚いた
義理人情に厚い男
とは聞いていたが
あれほどまでとは
思わなかった……

驚きましたね
あの男は平然と
女をとると
言い放ちました

Mm. That surprised me. I'd heard he was loyal and compassionate, but I didn't think he'd take it that far.

What a shocker. Calmly declaring he'd choose the woman …

俺も
そう思う

でも何だか
愛すべきキャラクター
じゃないですか？

I agree.

Still … You can't help but like a man with that sort of character.

臨時取締役会

We're here to
announce the
appointment of the
new president and
CEO. The chairman
and I have studied the
matter carefully and
come to a decision.

それでは　ただ今より
新社長人事の発表をいたします
これは私と会長とで
いろいろ検討いたしまして
決定いたしました

As the sixth president and CEO of Hatsushiba Electric, we have selected Mr. Kentaro Mangame.

So with no further ado ...

CLAP CLAP

CLAP CLAP CLAP CLAP CLAP

...

このことはすでに
一部の役員と一部の株主に
本日午前中に連絡して
諒解(りょうかい)を得ております

This morning we contacted certain board members and major shareholders and received their consent.

それでは
万亀君

Mr. Mangame.

正式発表は来年の決算役員会で行い
2月の株主総会で決定されますので
よろしくお願いいたします

It will be formally announced at the audit meeting next year and finalized at the meeting of shareholders in February.

はい

Thank you.

万亀で
ございます！

Mangame, at your service!

はい

RINNGGG

おめでとう
ございます！

あ　私だ……
先ほど社長に
選ばれた……

心配するな
俺達は今のままだ
自分の地位とひきかえに
おまえを棄てたりはしない

……私

SERIES8 II／
おわり

54

SUNSHINE Ⅲ

SWISH
SWISH

クリュ
クリュ

ん—

Mmm …

どうですか
味は？

Mitsugu Hanamori, section chief, wine division

ワイン事業部
課長
花森貢

How does it taste?

＊サンテミリオン……ボルドーの一地区の名称。特別級はこの地区において2番目の格付け。

うまい！

GULP

コロ
ッ
ク
ン

It's good!

ボルドー＊サンテミリオンの特別級
※※シャトー・パピヨンです

(* A fictional label)

It's Château Papillon*, a St-Emilion Grand Cru Classé Bordeaux.

テイスティングで
いちいち飲んでいたら
酔っ払いますよ

あー　また
飲んじゃった

If you swallow all the wine during a tasting you'll get drunk.

Ah! You swallowed again!

＊＊シャトー・パピヨン……このワインの品名・ラベルのデザインは架空のものです。

でしょ　だからここに
吐き出してくださいよ

味も
わからない

That's why
you should
spit it out.
In here.

うん　もう
いい気持ちになった

Can't
taste
a thing,
though

Yeah. I
already
feel
pretty
good.

売値は　'93年　'94年が
約1万円前後になります

＊メルロ種が50%はいって
いますので　かなり柔らかい感じで
飲みやすいと思います

The '93 and
'94 vintages
sell for about
10,000 yen.

It's 50%
Merlot, so
it's quite
soft and
smooth and
easy to
drink.

Shall we
move on?

いや　何か
勿体(もったい)なくて

I just
hate to
waste
it.

次
行きますか？

いや　もう勘弁してくれよ
これ以上　テイスティングすると
歩けなくなる

No, I've had
enough. Any
more
tasting and
I won't be
able to walk.

Ha, ha, ha!
Very well.

ハハハ
わかりました

＊メルロ種……赤ワインの原料となる葡萄の一種。

57

ふう

Phew.

PLOP

ウィッ

Whee.

WOBBLE WOBBLE

島専務
どうしました？
フラフラしてますよ

Are you all right, Mr. Shima? You're staggering.

いや……
新しく輸入するワインの
テイスティングをしていたら
酔っ払っちゃった

う〜〜〜
頭痛が

Ooh. My head hurts.

I got drunk tasting the new wines we're importing.

ところでキミは
ワインは好きか？

ありがと

はい
お水

Do you like wine, by the way?

Thanks.

Have some water.

58

今 勉強してるけど
ややこしくて……

I'm boning up now, but it's so complicated …

ハハハ 俺も
似たようなもんだ

Ha, ha! I'm about the same.

でも よくわかりません
赤と白の区別はつくけど

But I don't know much about it. I can tell red from white, but

はい
もちろん

Yes, of course.

ええ 定休日は
月曜日ですから
今日はオープンしてます

Yes. They're open every day except Monday.

あ そうだ!
新宿の伊勢屋デパートは
今日 やってるかなあ

Say! Is the Iseya department store in Shinjuku open today?

閉店は何時だっけ?

What time do they close?

うん ちょっと
本社に行った帰りに
ワイン売り場に
行ってみようかと思っている

7時ですけど……
行かれるんですか

市場調査

Market research, you know.

Yeah. After stopping at headquarters. I'd like to check out the wine department.

At 7:00 … Are you going there?

59

I won't be back today.

OK.

Well, I'm off.

So how's your "new territory"?

60

カカカ
ま
がんばってくれたまえ

Ha, ha, ha! Well, hang in there!

一夜漬けの勉強ですが
知識をたたきこんで
いるところです

I'm trying to cram a lot of knowledge into my head overnight.

はい とりあえずワイン部門を
重点的にまかせられて
いますけど……

Well, they've pretty much put me in charge of the wine division, but …

とりあえず まだ
ハッシバに籍を置いて 相談役として
ボケーッと暮らすことになった……

Meanwhile I'm staying on officially as a consultant—mostly daydreaming the hours away.

ところで私も
この部屋を使えるのは
今月いっぱいだ

By the way, I'll have to move out of this office by the end of the month.

うん あの人は まだ元気だし
何せ奥方が 個人では筆頭株主だ
影響力は依然として大きい

Yes. He's still full of energy, and what with his wife being the largest individual shareholder, he yields as much influence as ever.

では会長は
大泉さんのままですか……

And Mr. Oizumi will carry on as chairman?

こんなことなら もっと早く
引退すればよかったと思っている

Lately I've been thinking I should have retired even sooner.

ま ヒマも
いいもんだ

It's not bad having time on my hands.

… Is that so?

…………
そうですか

YEAR-END SALE–YAMAGUCHI PREF
RING OUT THE OLD–BARGAIN SA

はい　地下2階に
ございます

ワイン売り場は
何階ですか？

It's two floors down, on 2B.

Where's the wine section?

え ── と　我社(うち)が
扱っている銘柄は……

Let's see ... The brands we're importing are ...

何か
お探しですか？

May I help you?

あ　いや
ちょっと
見てるだけです

ハハハ

Heh, heh ...

Huh? Oh, no, I'm just looking.

ル・パン
あります？

あ　そうだ！

こっちのコーナーには
もう少し高級なものが
置いてありますけど……

その辺りは
テーブルワインですね

Do you have Le Pin?

Oh, that reminds me

The better wines are in this corner over here.

These are table wines.

ちょっとお聞きしますけど
'86年のル・バンは
いくらで売られているんですか？

いえ　うちには
置いてないですけど

ル・バンですか？

Could you possibly tell me how much a bottle of Le Pin '86 would be?

No, we don't carry it, but …

Le Pin?

そうですね　市場価格は
大体　1本14万円ぐらいだと思います

'86年のル・バンは
…………は

Yes, the retail price would be about 140,000 yen a bottle, I'd say.

Le Pin … vintage 1986 …

"チャコ" のママは
そんな高価なワインを
抜いてくれたのか…………

14万円 !!

The Mama-san at Chaco opened such an expensive wine for us?

140,000 yen!!

Here's to your new start!!

ちょっと高くついちゃうけど
ま　いいか……

新しい門出に
カンパーイ!!

This will set me back quite a bit, but … Oh, well.

Excuse me.

すみません

64

どうぞ
こちらへ

This way, please.

はい

Certainly!

10万円くらいの値段のワインを
ちょっと見せてくれませんか？

Could you show me some bottles priced around 100,000 yen?

1980

あ
じゃ
これを……

Well, let's try this one.

GRAND VIN DE CHATEAU LATOUR
1930

10万円前後となりますと
今 ここにあるのが ボルドーでは
※ラフィット ムートン ラトゥール
マルゴー それからトロタノワの'82年とか
シュヴァル・ブランの'90年 ブルゴーニュなら

In the 100,000-yen range we currently carry such Bordeaux wines as Lafite, Mouton, Latour, Margaux, Trotanoy '82, and Cheval Blanc '90. As for Burgundies …

これは最高の
ワインです

はい！ '90年の
ラトゥールですね

A superb choice!

Yes, sir! The Latour '90 …

すみませんが
これ プレゼント用に
つつんでくれますか

はい

Certainly.

Could you wrap it for me? It's a present.

*ラフィット、ムートン、ラトゥール、マルゴーはともに、第1級に格付けされているボルドー・メドック地区の5大シャトーのひとつ（もうひとつは、オー・ブリオン）。トロタノワもボルドーのポムロル地区のもので、高い評価を得ている。シュヴァル・ブランはサンテミリオン地区の第1特別級。

CLACK CLACK CLACK

あら！
島専務

Why, it's Mr. Shima!

!!

あ こりゃ
バッタリ会っちゃったね

Well, imagine bumping into you like this.

いや ちょっと
ゴールデン街のスナックに……

Ah, just to a little bar in Golden Lane …

ゴールデン街って
行ったことないな
一緒についていっても
いいですか？

えーッ
ゴールデン街の
スナックですかぁ

You don't say! A bar in Golden Lane?

I've never been to Golden Lane. Can I go with you?

You look awfully happy.

Where are you going?

何か
嬉しそうだわ

これから
どこへ
行かれるんですか？

I wonder who.

あ 誰かと待ち合わせなんだ！
お邪魔かしら

う うん
それは …………

だぁれかな

Oh, I guess I'd be in the way. You're meeting someone!

Ah …
Well …

ワ──
嬉しい‼

いいよ じゃ
一緒に行こう

いや そんなことは
ないさ……

Oh, goody‼

All right, you can come with me.

No, it's not that, but …

ハハハ
そうかな

うわ　なんか
あやしいところ

Ha, ha! Does it?

It looks kind of dodgy to me.

SHINJUKU GOLDEN

CREAK

CHACO

あら
お連れさま？

嬉しいわ　いつ　また
会えるのかと
ず——っと待っていたの

あ——ッ
島さん
いらっしゃい‼

Oh, you've brought a friend?

I was wondering when I'd see you again.

Mr. Shima! How nice! Welcome!

今晩は

うん　今日は私の秘書の
高市君を連れてきた

Hello.

This is my secretary, Miss Takaichi.

68

すごーい！！
'90年のラトゥール

今日は
そのお返しに
これをプレゼントするよ

ほら この間来た時
とても貴重なワインを
開けてもらったから

Oh, my! Latour '90!

So I brought you this in return.

Last time I was here you opened that valuable vine ...

SMACK

ありがとう！

CHU

Thank you!

おいおい
部下のいる前で
キスなんかされると
ちょっと困っちゃうな

Hey! Must you kiss me in front of my secretary?

うれしい
けど...！

I'm honored, but ...

69

What an annoying woman!

やな女

外国暮らしが長かったから
つい　向こうの習慣が
出ちゃった‼

I lived overseas for so long ... I'm afraid I forgot myself for a moment!

あ——ッ
ゴメンなさい‼

Oh! I'm sorry!

あなた　帰りたかったら
いつでも帰っていいのよ

Feel free to leave whenever you like.

まま
今日は楽しく飲もう！

Now, now, let's be nice and enjoy ourselves!

まさにこれが
とんでもない夜の
幕開けだった

This was just the beginning of a truly insane night.

SERIES8 III／おわり

70

SUNSHINE IV

CHACO

じゃ 次はブルゴーニュのワイン
飲んでみる？
ボルドーのワインとの
違いがわかると思うわ

口あたりも
いい

うん
これもうまい

Would you like to try a Burgundy next? I think you'll see how it differs from a Bordeaux.

Very pleasant on the palate.

Mmm. This is good, too.

Chaco

郵 便 は が き

112-8790

料金受取人払

小石川局承認

3049

差出有効期間
平成13年8月
5日まで

愛読者カード係

講談社バイリンガル・コミックス

インターナショナル　行

講談社

東京都文京区音羽一丁目

十七番十四号

ǁ|ll·|l·|lιιll·ιll·ιll·ι|ll·ιll·ι|l·ιll·ιll·|ll·|ll·ι|l·|l||

ａ．本書と、この「バイリンガル・コミックス」シリーズについ
て、お気づきの点、ご感想などをお教えください。（内容、体裁、
値段などについても、ご意見をお待ちしています）

お買い上げの「バイリンガル・コミックス」のタイトルをお書きください。

b　ご住所　　　　　　　　　　　　　　　〒□□□-□□□□

c　お名前　　　　　　　　　　　　d　年齢　（　　　）歳

　　　　　　　　　　　　　　　　　e　性別　1男性　2女性

f　ご職業　1大学生　2短大生　3高校生　4中学生　5各種学校生
　　　　　6教職員　7公務員　8会社員(事務系)　9会社員(技術系)　10会社役員
　　　　　11研究職　12自由業　13サービス業　14商工従事　15自営業　16農林漁業
　　　　　17主婦　18家事手伝い　19無職　20その他(　　　　　　　　　　)

g　この「バイリンガル・コミックス」をお選びいただいた理
　　由は何ですか。
　　　1このコミックスのファンだから
　　　2英語(英会話)の勉強になると思ったから
　　　3趣味、娯楽のため
　　　4その他(　　　　　　　　　　　　　　　　　　　　　)

h　この「バイリンガル・コミックス」を何で（どこで）お知
　　りになりましたか。

i　「バイリンガル・コミックス」で読みたいマンガ（日本・海
　　外）をあげてください。

j　どんなコミックスのノベルス（小説版）を英語で読みたい
　　ですか。

k　「講談社英語文庫」「講談社ルビー・ブックス」「講談社バイ
　　リンガル・ブックス」をご存じですか。ご存じでしたら、
　　読みたいタイトルをお教えください。

ご協力ありがとうございました。

何ていうのか
力強い感じがする

... It's ... how should I put this? More robust.

あ そうだね さっき飲んだ
ボルドーより少しフルーティーな
感じがするけど……

Oh, yeah. It seems a bit fruitier than the Bordeaux.

ビンの形

The shape of the bottle.

うん
わかった

Yeah.

どう お嬢さん？
ボルドーと
ブルゴーニュの違いがわかった？

Well, miss? Can you tell the difference between the Burgundy and the Bordeaux?

確かに
そのとおり

It's just as you say.

あ でもあなた
いいところに気づいたわね

Ah! You've raised a good point.

やな予感がする

I don't like where this is going.

これは
バカでもわかる
見分け方ね

... is square-shouldered. Any fool can see that.

ブルゴーニュのワインのビンは
なで肩タイプ
一方 ボルドーの方は いかり肩タイプ

Bottles of Burgundy have sloping shoulders. The Bordeaux, on the other hand ...

GRRR

ふーん
何か理由があるの？

うわ やばいな

ブルゴーニュのワインはボルドーより　もっと
澱が沈みにくいんだけど　澱引きと濾過(ろか)をするので
ビン詰める際に澱が入り込まないの
だからビンに肩を作る必要がないわけ

あるわよ　この肩の張りは澱(オリ)をとる機能があるの
つまり　ボルドーのワインは　澱が細かくて軽いので
ワインの中に浮遊しやすいの
だから注ぐ時に　この肩にひっかけるわけね

イカリ肩だし

じゃ
ママはボルドー形ね

へえ　そうなんだ
知らなかった……　形からみれば
ブルゴーニュのビンの方がセクシーだよね

帰って
ご自分で調べなさい

え？
それどんなビン？

あなたは※キアンティか……
あるいは※マグナムタイプね

あーら
ありがとう

※キアンティ……イタリアの赤ワインの名称。一般的にはワラで包んだフラスコ型のびんに詰められる。
※マグナム……ボルドーワインの、1.5ℓびん。ボルドーでは普通は750㎖のびんが用いられる。

3人で
合計5本ね

So it's 5 bottles between the three of us.

ボルドーを3本
ブルゴーニュを2本

Oh, 3 Bordeaux and 2 Burgundies

何本
空けた？

How many bottles is that?

Hic

ふう〜〜
ずいぶん飲んだな

Phew ... We've drunk quite a bit.

でもホラ おかげで
このうるさい秘書が
すっかりおとなしくなったわ

But just look. At least it quieted down your big-mouthed secretary.

Zzz

Zzz

うわ……
そりゃ
飲みすぎだ

Whoa ... That's overdoing it.

一番大きな違いっていうと……
やはり葡萄の品種だわね……

Well, the biggest difference would have to be the grapes ...

ところで ボルドーと
ブルゴーニュのワインの
大きな違いって 他に何か……

By the way, is there any other big difference between Bordeaux and Burgundies?

ハハハ
そうだな

Ha, ha! That's true.

ボルドーの赤ワインは　ベースとなる葡萄がカベルネ・ソーヴィニヨン
皮の色が黒くて　タンニンが多い品種なので　色の濃い
渋みの多いワインとなるのね　ただボルドーの場合　他の品種　メルロとか
カベルネ・フランといった葡萄をブレンドするのが一般的なのね

The grapes that are dominant in Bordeaux are the Cabernet Sauvignon. They're a dark-skinned variety with a high tannin content. They produce a deeply colored, rather astringent wine. But normally Bordeaux are blended with Merlot and Cabernet Franc varieties.

だから　ボルドーのワインは
各シャトーのブレンドのさじ加減で
味が決まるとも言えるのね

例えば　メルロ種をブレンドすれば
より柔らかくなり　カベルネ・フランを入れると
より軽くなるといった感じね

The varying proportions of each vineyard's blends determine the character of the wine.

Merlot contribute a softness and Cabernet Franc provide a lightness.

ウイスキーで言えば
シングルモルト

そう　ブルゴーニュは
ピノ・ノワールの
単一品種だけで作るのね

なるほど……
するとブルゴーニュの
赤ワインはブレンドしないの？

Kind of like single-malt whiskey.

Right. Burgundies are made from only one variety—Pinot Noir.

I see. But the red Burgundy wines don't employ a blend of grapes?

その葡萄が育つ畑の土壌で　味や香りが全然　違ってくるのね

そこが　ブルゴーニュワインの　凄いところよ

え？　すると　どこも同じ味に　なっちゃうんじゃないの？

ブルゴーニュ地方は　いろんな地層が入りくんだやせ地で出来ている
その土地で葡萄を栽培すると　葡萄の根は　水分と養分を求めて
地層の深いところ10メートルとか20メートルまで根をのばしてゆくのね
この地層の香りを葡萄がとり込むから　いろんな地層が
重なり合っているところほど　すばらしいワインが出来るというわけ

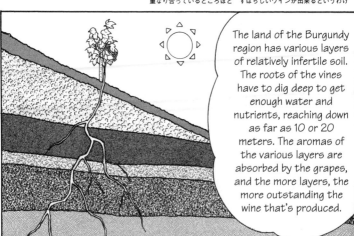

そうよ　現地へ行ってみるとわかるけど
葡萄の木は地面から直接　立ちあがっていて
高さは1.2メートルぐらいにおさえてあり
樹齢は30年から50年のものが多いので　幹も太いのよ……

へえ
葡萄といっても
日本のように棚にぶらさがっている
わけじゃないんだ……

その時　今日いただいた
'90年のラトゥールを
開けましょう！

I'll wait till then to open the Latour '90 you gave me tonight.

じゃ　帰って来たら
またこのお店に
寄ってね

Well, when you get back be sure to stop in here again.

うん　来週には
フランスへ行って
現地を視察してくるんだ

Actually, I'm going to France next week to look things over.

でも今度は一人で来てね
今　となりで寝ている
白ブタはいらないわ

But come alone next time. I can do without the pale little piggy sleeping next to you.

いいのよ　そんな
気をつかって
くれなくても

You don't have to do any such thing.

へえ　そりゃ嬉しいな……
じゃ　また何か新しい
ワインを買ってこなきゃ

Really? That's great … I'll have to find another interesting wine to bring.

おーい
高市君　帰るぞ

Takaichi. Hey! We're leaving.

Gngg

終電も
終わったな

The last train's gone by now.

あ　もう
こんな時間だ！

Whoa, look at the time!

ちょっと　お嬢さん　しっかりしなさい
上司にコートを着せてもらって
どうすんの！

Straighten up, young lady. Letting your boss put on your coat for you!

よし
コート着て！

Here's your coat.

ふわあ……
少し寝てたかもしれない

(Yawn.) I think I dozed off for a minute!

BARF

Gotta puke.

高市君！
Takaichi!

?

高市君
キミの家はどこだ？
Takaichi, where do you live?

うわ　大変な
ことになった
What a mess!

大丈夫か？
Are you OK?

Burrp

起きろ
Wake up!

Taka-ichi!

高市君！
Taka-ichi!

いかん！
眠ってる‼
Oh, no! She fell asleep!!

Zzz　Zzz

高市君！

HOTEL VENICE

仕方ない
ここに入るしかない……
No choice but to take her in here.

ZOOOT

Oof. She must weigh a ton.

しかし　また庭石のように
重い女だな

PLOP よっこいしょ

Oof.

なんでこんなことに
なるんだ……

Why do these things happen to me?

はいはい
わかりましたよ

Yes, ma'am. Just a moment.

水　苦しい

Water.

I'm dying …

お待たせ

Here you …

GLOOP GLOOP

こんな場所に
長居は出来ない
ホテル代だけ置いて
先に帰ろう……

I can't stay here long. I'll pay for the room and leave.

81

うわ

Aggh!

来て!! ね!!
私を抱いて!!

Come!!
Take
me!!

···

!!

高市君　待ってくれ！
そんなことはダメだ
私には部下を抱く意思は
ないから

Takaichi,
wait! Stop
it! I can't
sleep with
my
secretary!

PLOP

You just threw up!

だ……
だめだよ
そんなこと

キスと
言われても……

じゃ
キスして

No way!

さっきゲロした
ままの口で……

Kiss you?

Kiss me, then.

う……
うん
それなら

じゃ このまま
しばらく
抱いててくれる？

Well, I ...
I guess.

Then will you just hold me awhile?

Zzz

とんでもないことに
なっちゃったな

Zzz   Zzz

!?

What an insane situation.

ちょうどいい
今のうちに
そっと帰ろう

あー また
眠っちゃったよ

Perfect. I'll slip out now.

Asleep again!

84

高市君の方から
何か言わない限り
このことは黙っていよう

I won't say anything unless she brings it up.

どう考えを
整理したらいいのか
わからないが
とにかく これは現実だ

I don't know what to make of this, but there it is.

翌日

The next day ...

あ どうも
ありがとう

Oh, thanks.

おはようございます
来週からのフランス出張の
チケットが来ましたので
お渡しします

Good morning! Your ticket to France has arrived.

あ
もちろん

このことは絶対
内緒にして下さい
お願いします!!

You mustn't tell anyone. Please!!

Of course.

う
うん……
まあ

Er ... Yeah.

私の背中……
見ちゃいましたよね?

専務 昨日はいろいろと
すみませんでした
すべて なかったことに
して下さい

You saw my back, didn't you?

Sorry about last night. Please pretend it didn't happen.

だけど……

ひとつだけ聞かせてくれ　どうして　彫り物なんか入れたんだ？

あれは　私が高校生の時に　父の方から入れろって　言うから　入れたんです

今じゃ　とても後悔　してるけど……

お父さんが？　……

どうして？

私の父は　ヤクザの組長なの

これも　内緒！

…………
わかりました

SUNSHINE V

CLACK CLOP   CLACK CLOP

PERSONNEL DEPARTMENT

あ　島専務
何か？

Yes, Mr. Shima?

私の秘書の
高市君だ

My secretary, Ms. Takaichi.

何か問題でも
ありましたか？

Is there some problem?

少々
お待ち下さい

One moment, please.

TAP TAP

よろしいですよ
どなたですか？

Yes, sir. Which one?

うん
ちょっと社員の
個人データを
見せて欲しいんだ

I'd like to see the file on one of our employees.

88

いや 別に
そういうことではないんだが
彼女に対して 何も
予備知識がないものでね

はい
出ました
どうぞ！

ありがとう！

Thanks.

Here's the printout.

No, nothing in particular. I just don't have any background info on her.

高市千鶴
昭和48年6月6日生まれ
聖清女子中学校　聖清女子学園
聖清女子大学英文科卒
英検1級取得　趣味はゴルフ

現住所
東京都世田谷区成城××丁目×ー×

Home address:
XX-X-X Seijo,
Setagaya-ku,
Tokyo

なるほど　ここまでは
典型的なお嬢様といった
経歴だな

Hmm ...
Nothing here
to distinguish
her from your
typical upper-
middle class
young lady ...

Chizuru Takaichi

Date of Birth: June 6, 1973

• Education: Seisei Women's Middle School
Seisei Women's High School
Seisei Women's College—graduated with a major in English literature
Qualifications: First-level English proficiency certificate

• Hobbies: Golf

現住　東京都　世田谷区　成城

右側は
私の誕生日
いれていいですか？

じゃ左は
9・0・9……と

私は
9月9日生まれだ

SPIN SPIN

私は6月6日生まれだから
6・0・6……
忘れないで下さいね

いいとも

You nasty man!
Ha, ha, ha!

Mr. Shima! I know
what you're thinking!

右が6・0・6
左が9・0・9

バレたか！

それは
オマエだろ

91

えー　現在　ウチが扱っております
※シャトー・パピヨン
シャトー・モンク
シャトー・ジャルダン等の
昨年の売り上げグラフです

This graph shows last year's sales of the wines we're importing: Château Papillon, Château Monk, Château Jardin,* and so on.

(* All fictional labels)

あと　チリ
アルゼンチンのワインも
好調ですね

そうですね　最近では
女性の方のブルゴーニュ派が
増えています

売れ筋はやはり
ボルドーか……

Wines from Chile and Argentina are also doing well.

Yes, sir. But female consumers are increasingly favoring Burgundy.

Sure enough, the Bordeaux are moving, then …

*これらのワインの銘柄は架空のものです

92

チリ・アルゼンチンは唯一
ヨーロッパ種の葡萄の木が
残ってますから

After all, Chile and Argentina are the only countries that still have European vines.

はい 値段の割には
すばらしいものが
たくさんあります

There are many excellent labels for the price.

最近 チリワインの人気が
高いですが
品質はどうですか？

Chilean wines are very popular recently. How's the quality?

現存しているのは
アメリカから持ってきた品種を 台木にして
接(つ)ぎ木して育てたもので
従来のヨーロッパ種は南米にしかありません

The vines there now were created by grafting onto rootstocks brought over from the U.S. The true European varieties now exist only in South America.

実はフランスの葡萄は
19世紀後半にヨーロッパを
襲った害虫にやられて
ほぼ全滅したんです

Actually, the vines in France fell victim to a harmful insect that destroyed most European vineyards in the latter half of the 19th century.

え？ すると
フランスの葡萄は？

What? And the vines in France?

今 フランスのワインが飲めるのは
アメリカのおかげとも言えるんだ

So you might say we have America to thank for the French wines we drink now.

へえ……
それは知らなかったな

I'll be ... I didn't know that.

現在は世界中の輸入業者が複雑に
はいりこんできてますから
独占というのは 極めて難しいですね

Importers from around the globe are involved now. It's a complicated system, and getting exclusive rights would be extremely difficult.

どこかのワイナリーと組んで
独占して販売することが
出来ないのかな

Can't we link up with some winery to get exclusive selling rights?

もっとも
独占販売契約に成功しても
売れなければ意味はないですからね

But of course it wouldn't do us much good if the wine didn't sell.

独占するなら
新しいシャトーで
規模の小さいものなら
可能でしょう

It might be possible to get exclusive rights to the wines of some new, small château …

人気のあるワインには
輸入業者が殺到します
例えば'83年ものに3社
'90年ものに5社
といったぐあいですね

Importers flock to the more popular wines. For example, 3 companies for the 1983 vintage, 5 for the 1990 vintage, and so on.

むしろ在庫を抱えて
赤字を出してしまうことに
なるでしょう

We'd end up over-stocked and suffering a loss.

どうして

Why's that?

独占的な契約なら
ブルゴーニュのワインの方が
とりやすいんじゃないでしょうか

It would probably be easier to obtain exclusive rights on Burgundies.

大雑把(おおざっぱ)に言えば
ブルゴーニュは葡萄栽培者と製造業者が
バラバラであるということです

Speaking in broad terms, the growers and the producers of Burgundies are separate.

ワイン製造の
システムの違いです

Because of the different system of production.

ボルドーの場合は
シャトーがあって　その周辺の葡萄畑をシャトーが所有して
そこで栽培された葡萄をシャトーの工場でワインにする
――つまり一から十まで　そのシャトーが行うというのが一般的です

In the case of Bordeaux, there's a château that owns the surrounding vineyard. The grapes grown there are processed at the château's own winery. In other words, the château generally does it all, from start to finish.

葡萄畑を所有し　栽培　醸造ビン詰めを行う生産者を
ドメーヌと呼び ※主に他人の畑から
葡萄を買いとって　熟成　販売　輸出までを行う業者を
ネゴシアン・エルヴールといいます

一方　ブルゴーニュの場合はとても複雑で
一口で説明しきれませんが　葡萄畑の所有者と栽培者
ワインの製造者と販売業者が　それぞれ独立しているんです
そして　これらのいくつかを兼ねているものもあります

A producer that owns the vineyard, cultivates the vines, and makes and bottles the wine is called a domaine. A dealer who buys up the grapes from other vineyards, ages, sells, and even exports the wine, is called a négociant-éleveur.

It's much more complex for Burgundies, too complex to explain briefly, but the owners of the vineyards, the growers, the winemakers, and the shippers are often all independent of one another. And there's a certain amount of overlap.

ブルゴーニュの40%は
ドメーヌもので
60%がネゴシアンもの
といった比率です

ドメーヌというのは
ボルドーで言うところの
シャトーとほぼ同じと
考えていいでしょう

何だか　よく
わからなくなったな

Something like 40% of Burgundies are from domaines and 60% are handled by négociants.

A domaine is more or less the same as what we call a château in the case of Bordeaux.

You lost me.

※自分の畑をもつネゴシアン・エルヴールもある。

そういうのが見つかると
ラッキーですね

ということは　非常に上質なワインを
小さな規模でこぢんまりと作っている
ドメーヌもあるということです

更にブルゴーニュの畑には
きわめて多くの権利者が錯綜(さくそう)していて
ひとうねごとに所有者が違う畑もあります

With luck, we might find one of those.

Which means that there are some domaines that produce exceptionally high quality Burgundies on a very small scale.

What's more, ownership rights to Burgundy vineyards are extremely complicated. Some vineyards even have different owners for each row of vines.

確かにそれは
とても難しいと思います

見つけても　果たして日本の業者と
独占契約を結んでくれるかどうか　問題だな

I'm sure it wouldn't be easy.

But even if we found one, who's to say we could get them to sign an exclusive contract with a Japanese firm?

そして　うまく交渉してくれる
仲買人をみつけることが
大変重要ですね

ブルゴーニュには　クールティエと呼ばれる
仲買人の存在がありますので
まず目利きの仲買人をみつけること

And who could do a good job of negotiating for us.

In Burgundy they have brokers known as courtiers. First we'd have to find a courtier with impeccable judgment ...

いずれにしても　独占契約より　まず
日本で売れるワインを輸入することを
考えた方が得策かと思います

うーん
こりゃ　やっぱり
無理か

In any case, exclusive rights aside, we first need to concentrate on finding wines that will sell well in Japan.

Hmm. I suppose it's pretty hopeless, then.

We will be temporarily
closed for some time.
– The owner

どうしたんだろう
体調でも悪いのか
あるいは
長期の旅行にでも
出かけたか

I wonder
what
happened.
Maybe
she's ill.
Or off on
a long trip
somewhere
…

都合により
しばらくの間
閉店させて頂きます。

店主

え？ 閉店

Closed?

成田空港

じゃ
行ってくる

そろそろ
ゲートにはいった方が
よさそうだな

Well, I'd better get to the gate.

See you, then.

...

DRIP DROP

そのカバンを
こっちにくれ

Hand me my attaché case.

?

SNATCH

私もついて
いきたーい

I want to go with you!

お　おい髙市君
やめろ
みんなが見てるぞ

Takaichi, stop it. Everyone's looking.

Don't leave me!

やだあ
離れたくなーい！

SQUEEZE

99

FWOOOOSSSSHH

彼女の行動パターンが
全く読めない
ソラ恐ろしい女だ

You can't predict her behavior at all. Kind of scary.

ふう 全くあいつ
何を考えてるんだ

Phew. What the hell is she thinking?

SNAP

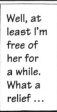

ま しかし
しばらくは
会うこともないので
ホッとするな……

Well, at least I'm free of her for a while. What a relief …

一体次はどんな
エキセントリックな
行動に出るかと思うと
心臓に悪い

Puts a strain on my heart wondering what her next weird stunt will be.

え？

Huh?

XOXO!

何だ？
これは !?

FROM CHIZURU WITH LOVE

パリで淋(さみ)しくなったら
これで私を思い出してね
千鶴

What is this?

島耕作様
コレさっきまで　はいていました
トイレで脱いで
こっそり　しのばせたんです

If you get lonely in Paris, please use them to remember me by.
Chizuru

Dear Mr. Shima,
I was wearing these until just now. I took them off in the ladies' room and slipped them in here.

……たく！

そうか　あいつ俺の
カバンを開ける
暗証番号を
知ってるんだ

Good grief!

That's right, she knows the combination to my attaché case.

101

...

あ
シャンペンを
下さい

Oh!
Champagne,
please.

Heh,
heh ...

ハハハ

夕方には
パリに着く

We'll reach
Paris in
the late
afternoon.

END OF PART V

当機はあと30分ほどで
パリ シャルルドゴール空港へ
到着致します
現地の天候は晴れ 気温は…………

We'll be landing at
Charles de Gaulle Airport
in about 30 minutes. The
weather is fair in Paris;
the temperature is …

お休み中
申し訳ございませんが

Sorry to
disturb you,
sir …

まもなく着陸態勢にはいりますので
お座席を元の位置まで
お戻しになって下さい

We'll be preparing to
land soon. Please
put your seatback in
the upright position

Oh.
Right.

あ はい

WHOOOOSSSSHH

あ 島さんですね
お連れ様が先に
おはいりになっております

Yes, Mr. Shima. Your companion has already checked in.

予約している
島と申します

My name's Shima. I have a reservation.

あ あのう……
私は1人で予約している
はずですが

I ... I believe I reserved a room for only one ...

連れ？

Companion?

KLATCH

昨日 キャンセルがありまして
2人宿泊になっております
お連れ様のサインはここに……

There was a cancellation yesterday, and you have a room for two now. Here's the signature.

クミコ・オオマチ……

Kumiko Omachi ...

だって明日から
アランが合流するのよ
2人きりになれるのは
今夜だけだもの

Well, Alain will join us tomorrow. Tonight's our only chance to be alone.

何も知らされて
なかったから
ちょっと
びっくりしたぞ

This is quite a surprise. You didn't tell me anything.

だから　そのぶん
思い切り
楽しみましょう

Let's make the most of it.

109

島さん

Hey …

What?

何……

私　1年分いっちゃったから
これでしばらく
してくれなくても　大丈夫

Har-har.

なーんてね

I just had a year's worth of orgasms. No need to do it for a while …

50歳を越えると　その気違いが
とてもうれしいな　なーんてね

When you're over 50 you're grateful for such consideration … Har-har.

ハハハ
久しぶりに会うと
どうしても
そうなっちゃうな

何か私達
どこか照れてない？

Do we seem a little shy with each other?

Ha, ha! That's what happens when you don't meet for a long time.

AHHHHHHH

110

What was on the agenda for tomorrow again?

明日からの予定は
どうなってるんだっけ？

翌日は
国内線の飛行機で
ブルゴーニュへ行くわ

それからレンタカーを借りて
ボルドーのメドック地方を
ドライブするの

とりあえず　モンパルナス駅で
アランと合流して　3人で
※TGVでボルドーに行くわ

The next day we'll catch a plane to Burgundy.

Then we'll rent a car and drive to the Médoc region.

We'll meet Alain at Montparnasse Station and take the TGV to Bordeaux.

かなり　ハードな
スケジュールだな

Pretty hard schedule.

うん　とりあえず
このワインを飲んでから
考えよう

今夜のスケジュールも
ハードにしたいわね

We'll discuss that after we've drunk this wine.

I'd like tonight's schedule to be hard, too.

*TGV……フランスの新幹線。パリを起点に各地方に伸びている。日本の新幹線と違い、在来線に乗り入れできる。

島です
よろしく

初めまして
アランです

Shima. Nice to meet you.

How do you do? I'm Alain.

アラン・クレモン
初芝電産貿易パリ支社長

ええ　パリ大学で
日本語を専攻して
そのあと日本の銀行で
3年働きました

ずいぶん日本語が
達者ですね

Alain Clement, general manager of the Paris office of Hatsushiba Trading

I majored in Japanese at Paris University. After that I worked 3 years at a Japanese bank.

Your Japanese is excellent!

あら　島専務
私だってフランス語が
得意なんですよ
いつでも使って下さい

そうですか
それなら安心だ
私はフランス語は
さっぱりなんだ

But, Mr. Shima, French is my forte. Feel free to use it whenever you like, Alain.

Is that so? What a relief. I have no French at all.

WHOOOSH

※いや　新幹線より
速いでしょう

うわ　速いな
日本の新幹線なみだ

Even faster, I think.

Boy, this is as fast as the Shinkansen!

THUMP

このワインを
ご存じですか？

SNAP

ところで
島専務
早速ですが

Are you familiar with this wine?

Well. Getting right down to business ...

*TGVは最高時速300kmで営業運転している区間がある。日本の新幹線も、500系「のぞみ」は、時速300kmで運転している。

113

ボルドーのワインの中で
一番高いクラスのものです

It's in the highest class of Bordeaux.

そうです ボルドーの
ポムロル地区が生んだ 20世紀の
奇跡と呼ばれる傑作ワインです

That's right. A masterpiece produced in the Pomerol district of Bordeaux. They call it the miracle of the 20th century.

ペトリュス

Pétrus

うん すごく高価な
ワインだ

Very expensive, isn't it?

いや……
わからない

No. Why?

それが今や 1本数十万円……
何故(なぜ)でしょう

... tens of thousands of yen. Do you know why?

実はペトリュスは ほんの20年前は
大したことのないワインだったんです

But only 20 years ago, Pétrus was just another wine. Now a bottle goes for ...

その後 彼はシャトーの所有者の死後
株を買い占めて
製造 経営に参加していった……

After the death of the château's owner, he bought a half-share in the château and lent a hand in production and management.

ペトリュスは1945年に
ムエックスという商人が
買い占めてベルギーに
持ち込み 評判を呼びました

In 1945 a merchant named Moueix got exclusive selling rights to Pétrus and shipped it to Belgium. It proved a great hit there.

今から開けますから
ちょっと飲んでみて下さい

Let me open it and we'll have a taste.

なるほど……
まず市場を独占したわけだ

I see ... So first he monopolized the market.

参考資料……「BRUTUS」'96年10月15日号掲載の記事「『ペトリュスの奇跡』を生んだポムロル地区の不思議」(文・立石敏雄氏)

なあに
3人で銀座に行ったと思えば
大したことはありません

No different than if the three of us went to Ginza. Think of it that way.

Good point.

なんか
昼間から
すごく豪勢だな

Drinking wine in the middle of the day. What a luxury.

確かに

いかがですか？

How is it?

時間がたてば
もっとまろやかに
なります

It becomes even rounder with time.

でしょ！　ペトリュスは
メルロ種という葡萄を
95％以上使っているからです

Well put! Pétrus is made of a blend containing at least 95% Merlot grapes.

女優で言えば
カタセ・リノの
ような……

One might call it the Rino Katase of wines.

うん
丸味のある口あたり
豊かでなめらか……

Mm. Well-rounded, full-bodied, and smooth…

ペトリュスは1977年に今のメルロ95％になりましたが
それまでは、メルロ70％　カベルネ・フラン30％
というブレンドだったんですね

実はこれも　ムエックスが1964年にベルーエという
天才醸造家を※シェフ・ド・カーヴとして呼んで
配合を変えたからです

In 1977, the blend was changed from 70% Merlot and 30% Cabernet Franc to 95% Merlot.

Moueix was responsible for this, too. In 1964 he hired a brilliant winemaker named Berrouet to serve as his chef de cave, or oenologist, and experimented with the blend.

※シェフ・ド・カーヴ……カーヴはワインの貯蔵蔵のこと。シェフ・ド・カーヴはその責任者。

それを発見したので
余計なカベルネ・フランを
排除していった……

ペトリュスの畑は　他のポムロルの畑の
土壌とは違った　鉄分の多い粘土質でした
これがメルロ種と絶妙の相性を示したんです

へえ……何故？

When they discovered this, they eliminated the Cabernet Francs …

The vineyard that produces Pétrus is unlike that of others in Pomerol in that it has a clay soil with a high iron content. A superb match for Merlot grapes.

Hm … Why?

あと　後押しする
強力な鑑定家の
意見ですね

なるほど　すると
希少性と醸造家の技術があれば
奇跡をおこすことが出来るというわけか

That, and a powerful critic to get behind your wine.

I see. So with rare conditions and a skillful winemaker, you can produce a miracle.

例えば　ル・パン……以前は'82年ものが
1本100フラン（約2千円）で買えたのに
パーカーの評価を得るやいなや　ぐんぐん値上がりした……

そのとおり　ロバート・パーカーとか
ヒュー・ジョンソンのような高名な鑑定家が
高い評価を下すと　一晩で値上がりする世界なんです

Take Le Pin, for example. At one time you could buy a bottle of the 1982 vintage for 100 francs, or about 2000 yen. No sooner had Parker extolled it than the price shot up …

Exactly. This is a world in which, if a famous wine critic like Robert Parker or Hugh Johnson praises a wine highly, the price can skyrocket overnight.

すごい世界だな……

今や　1本55万円の
値がついてます

Good heavens!

Now a bottle goes for 550,000 yen.

ボルドー駅

我々ハツシバとしては
これを狙いたいわけです
ただ購入して販売するだけではなく
投機をしてみたいと思うわけです

That's what we at Hatsushiba Trading should aim for. Not just buying and selling; I think we should find a good wine to speculate on.

I see ... I wonder if we could pull it off.

なるほど……
うまくいくかな

ま それはムリでしょう
それが簡単にいけば
誰でもそうしてる

何じゃ
そりゃ……

What the ...?

Probably not. If it were that easy, everyone would do it.

ボルドーはブルゴーニュと並んで フランスを代表するワインの産地で
フランス南西部のガロンヌ川 ジロンド川 ドルドーニュ川の両岸に
10万ヘクタールの葡萄畑が広がる

Along with Burgundy, Bordeaux is France's greatest wine-producing region. Vineyards cover 100,000 hectares along the banks of the Garonne, Gironde, and Dordogne Rivers in southwest France.

我々はボルドーからレンタカーを使って マルゴー サン・ジュリアン
ポイヤック サンテステフの村々をドライブした
この辺りはボルドーの最高のワインを産出する地区だ

We drove a rental car to the villages of Margaux, Saint-Julien, Pauillac, and Saint-Estèphe, in the district that produces the finest Bordeaux wines.

And another.

うわぁ
あそこにも

一面の葡萄畑の中を走ってゆくと 眼前に次々と
美しいシャトーが出現しては消える ボトルのエチケット
（ラベル）に描かれてある あのお馴染みのシャトーだ

Look, there's another one.

あそこにも

Driving through the sea of vineyards, one beautiful château after another bobbed up before our eyes. All with names familiar to us from the labels of famous wines.

Here, too.

シャトー・マルゴー

本来なら ここら一面
青々とした葡萄畑なんですけど
今は葉が落ちて
剪定(せんてい)されてるから
何か殺風景ですね

こうして見ると
冬の葡萄畑って
日本の桑畑にも似てるな

A vineyard in winter … Kind of reminds me of the mulberry orchards back in Japan.

It's green as far as the eye can see during growing season. But now that all the leaves have fallen and the vines are being pruned, it's not so beautiful.

あ
シャトー・パルメが
見えるわ

アハハ
面白い発想ですね

Oh, look! You can see Château Palmer!

Ha, ha! That's an interesting thought.

Château Pichon-
Longueville

Château Léoville-
Las-Cases

シャトー・レオヴィル・
ラス・カーズ

シャトー・ピション・
ロングヴィル

シャトー・コス・
デストゥルネル

Château Cos
d'Estournel

あれは
仲買人(クールティエ)
ですよ

いちいち土を拾って
つぶしてみたり
口に含んだりしている

何だろう
あの男

He's a courtier.

He's picking up bits of soil, crushing them, and tasting the dirt.

Who would that be?

彼等は　情報が命ですから
どんな小さなシャトーやドメーヌも
自分の足でまわり　味を確かめておくんですね
いわばプロ中のプロです

ワインが　生産者から※ネゴシアン（卸商）に
渡る間に彼等(かれら)がいるんです
売買が成立した時には　仲買人は双方から
約3％の手数料をとる――
そういう商売ですね

Information is vital to them, so they visit each château or domaine, no matter how small, and make sure the conditions are right. They're the pros among the pros.

They stand between the wine producers and the négociants. When a sale is made, the courtier receives a 3% commission from each ... That's their business.

※ネゴシアン……ワインを大量に買いあつめ、調合してびん詰めし、国内外に売り出す業者のこと。ネゴシアンの中には
自分の葡萄畑を所有し、熟成も行う者もおり、彼らはネゴシアン・エルヴールと呼ばれる。

ボンジュール

この男が後に
どんなに深く
係わってくるかは
この時点では
誰もわからなかった……

ボンジュール
マドモアゼル

STEP18／おわり　　　　TO BE CONTINUED

講談社バイリンガル・コミックス

バイリンガル版 部長 島耕作 ③
DIVISION CHIEF KOSAKU SHIMA ③

2000年7月14日　第1刷発行

著　者　　弘兼憲史

訳　者　　ラルフ・マッカーシー

発行者　　野間佐和子

発行所　　講談社インターナショナル株式会社
　　　　　〒112-8652　東京都文京区音羽1-17-14
　　　　　電話：03-3944-6493（編集部）
　　　　　　　　03-3944-6492（営業部・業務部）

印刷所　　株式会社廣済堂

製本所　　株式会社廣済堂

ISBN4-7700-2635-8

講談社バイリンガル・コミックス

吹き出しのセリフは英語、コマの外にオリジナル版の日本語を添えた
画期的なレイアウトで、原作のもつ雰囲気と面白さはそのまま。楽し
く読みながら英語の勉強になる！　　46判変型（113 x 188 mm）仮製

元気いっぱい、さくらちゃんです。英語でもおもろいで〜

バイリンガル版 カードキャプターさくら
Cardcaptor Sakura

CLAMP 著

第 1 巻　　　192ページ　　　ISBN 4-7700-2644-7

国内にとどまらず海外でも大人気の「金田一君」

バイリンガル版 金田一少年の事件簿
The New Kindaichi Files

金成陽三郎 原作　　さとうふみや 漫画

第1巻	オペラ座館殺人事件	192ページ	ISBN 4-7700-2599-8
第2巻	異人館村殺人事件	192ページ	ISBN 4-7700-2600-5
第3巻	雪夜叉伝説殺人事件	176ページ	ISBN 4-7700-2601-3
第4巻	雪夜叉伝説殺人事件・解決編	160ページ	ISBN 4-7700-2669-2

ドラマ、アニメ、映画と絶好調の「鬼塚先生」

バイリンガル版 GTO
Great Teacher Onizuka

藤沢とおる 著

第 1 巻	192ページ	ISBN 4-7700-2602-1
第 2 巻	192ページ	ISBN 4-7700-2603-X
第 3 巻	192ページ	ISBN 4-7700-2604-8

恋も仕事も絶好調！ ムリなく楽しく英語が話せる

バイリンガル版 部長 島耕作
Division Chief Kosaku Shima

弘兼憲史 著

第 1 巻	176ページ	ISBN 4-7700-2633-1
第 2 巻	128ページ	ISBN 4-7700-2634-X
第 3 巻	128ページ	ISBN 4-7700-2635-8

講談社バイリンガル・コミックス

バカが読んでも英語なのだ

バイリンガル版 天才バカボン
The Genius Bakabon

赤塚不二夫 著

アラ、こんなに楽しくて、ごめんあそばせ。英語で笑う

対訳 サザエさん
The Wonderful World of Sazae-san

長谷川町子 著

英語でOLしてみない !?

対訳 OL進化論
Survival in the Office

秋月 りす 著

新シリーズ登場!

バイリンガル版 あさきゆめみし
バイリンガル版 ラブひな

実用英語の総合シリーズ

- 旅行・留学からビジネスまで、コミュニケーションの現場で役立つ「実用性」
- ニューヨーク、ロンドンの各拠点での、ネイティブ チェックにより保証される「信頼性」
- 英語の主要ジャンルを網羅し、目的に応じた本選びができる「総合性」

46判変型（113 x 188 mm）仮製

1 これを英語で言えますか？　学校で教えてくれない身近な英単語

講談社インターナショナル 編　　　　　232ページ　ISBN 4-7700-2132-1

「ブランコ、鉄棒、すべり台」「短縮ダイヤル」「○×式テスト」「$a^2 + b^3 = c^4$」「円の面積は π 掛ける半径の2乗」「いない、いない、ばー」…これらを英語で言えますか？　本書は日本人英語の盲点に78の分野から迫ります。

2 遠山顕の英会話・150のスパイス　ムリなく使える決まり文句

遠山 顕 著　　　240ページ ISBN 4-7700-2586-6　CD(70分) 別売 ISBN 4-7700-2587-4

「一杯いこうか？」「なるようになりますよ」「テコでも動きませんよ」など、欧米人の会話にもしばしば使われる決まり文句150を、"やさしい""短い"をポイントに、選りすぐって紹介。すべて具体的な用例付きで応用も自由自在の、会話のスパイス集。

3 アメリカ旅行「使える」キーワード　場面別想定問答集

アンドリュー・ホルバート 著　　　　　240ページ　ISBN 4-7700-2481-9

出国から帰国まで、アメリカ旅行のすべてをカバーする一冊。ショッピングや食事、レンタカーの借り方からトラブル対処法まで様々な状況で必要となる決め手のフレーズ。そんな「コトバ」と、初心者でも楽しく旅ができる実用的な「情報」を満載。

4 ダメ！ その英語［ビジネス編］　日本人英語NG集

連東孝子 著　　　　　176ページ　ISBN 4-7700-2469-X

社長賞を貰ったアメリカ人の同僚に "You are lucky!" と言ってはダメ!?　ビジネスの場面を中心に、コミュニケーションの行き違い110例を紹介・解説。「この英語、なぜいけないの？」「どうして通じないの？」に答える、日本人英語のウィークポイント攻略本。

5 米語イディオム600　ELTで学ぶ使い分け＆言い替え

バーバラ・ゲインズ 著　　　　　208ページ　ISBN 4-7700-2461-4

イディオムを使いこなせるかどうかが英会話上達の決め手！　本書は「勘定を払う」「仕事を探す」など、日常生活に即した80の場面別に600以上の重要イディオムを紹介。ただ機械的に暗記するのではなく、状況に応じた言い替え・使い分けがマスターできる。

6 どこまで使える？ "go"と"come"　かんたん単語55の英会話

田崎清忠 著　　　　　208ページ　ISBN 4-7700-2527-0

"come" "take" "leave" など、中学校で習う初歩的な単語も、使い方次第で表現力が大幅アップ！　誰もが知っている簡単な単語55の意味と使い方を、肩の凝らないエッセイを通して紹介。つい見落としがちな、意味と用法の意外なバリエーションが気軽に学べる。

7 アメリカ留学日常語事典　これがなければ1日も過ごせない！

東照二 著　　　　　192ページ　ISBN 4-7700-2470-3

アメリカのキャンパスには、独特の用語や表現がいっぱいあります。本書は、留学を志す人、アメリカのキャンパスで生活する人が知っていないと困る用語と情報を一挙にまとめて、日本人にわかりやすく解説しました。

8 マナー違反の英会話　英語にだって「敬語」があります

ジェームス・M・バーダマン、森本豊富 共著　　208ページ　ISBN 4-7700-2520-3

英語にだって「敬語」はあります。「アメリカ人はフランクで開放的」と言われていますが、お互いを傷つけないように非常に気配りをしています。しかし親しい仲間うちで丁寧な英語表現ばかりを使っていては、打ち解けられません。英語にだってTPOがあります。

9 英語で「四字熟語」365　英語にするとこんなにカンタン！

松野守峰、N・ミナイ 共著　　272ページ　ISBN 4-7700-2466-5

四字熟語をマスターし、その英語表現によってボキャブラリーも急増する一石二鳥のおトクな1冊！　日常よく使われる365の四字熟語を「努力・忍耐」「チームワーク」「苦境」「性格」「能力」「友情」「恋愛」「宿命」などの意味別に分類し、英語にしました。

10 「英語モード」で英会話　これがネイティブの発想法

脇山怜、佐野キム・マリー 共著　　224ページ　ISBN 4-7700-2522-X

日本では、へりくだって相手を持ち上げることが処世術。しかし、「未経験で何もわかりませんがよろしく」のつもりで "I am inexperienced and I don't know anything." なんて英語圏で言えば、それはマイナスイメージ。英語でコミュニケーションをするときは、日本語から英語へ「モード」のスイッチを切り替えましょう。

11 英語で読む「科学ニュース」　話題の知識を英語でGet！

松野守峰 著　　208ページ　ISBN 4-7700-2456-8

科学に関する知識とことばが同時に身につく、画期的な英語実用書！「ネット恐怖症族」「スマート・マウスパッド」から「デザイナー・ドラッグ」「DNAによる全人類の祖先解明」まで、いま話題の科学情報が英語でスラスラ読めるようになります。

12 CDブック 英会話・ぜったい・音読　頭の中に英語回路を作る本

國弘正雄 編　千田潤一 トレーニング指導　　144ページ CD(40分)付　ISBN 4-7700-2459-2

英語を身につけるには、英語の基礎回路を作ることが先決です。英語を身体で覚える…、それには、何と言っても音読です。本書には、中学3年生用の英語教科書から、成人の英語トレーニングに適した12レッスンを厳選して収録しました。だまされたと思って、まずは3ヵ月続けてみてください。確かな身体の変化にきっと驚かれることでしょう。

13 英語のサインを読む　アメリカ生活情報早わかりマニュアル

清地恵美子 著　　240ページ　ISBN 4-7700-2519-X

広告や看板の読み方がわかると、アメリカの英語と暮らしが見えてきます。「スーパーのチラシに$2.99Lb.とあるけど」、「コインランドリーを使いたいのだけれど」。本書では自動販売機の使い方、案内板や利用説明書の読み方など、生活情報入手のコツを紹介します。

14 産直！ ビジネス英語　NY発、朝から夜までの英会話

藤松忠夫 著　　224ページ　ISBN 4-7700-2458-4

英語がペラペラしゃべれるだけでは、NYでビジネスは出来ません。会議を司会する、人事考課の評定を部下に納得させる、ビジネスランチを成功させる、効果的に情報を入手するなど……。これらが英語でちゃんと出来て、あなたは初めて一人前です。それには、アメリカ人の常識・習慣・考え方を知ったうえで適切な英語表現を身につけることが欠かせません。

15 A or B？ ネイティブ英語　日本人の勘違い150パターン

ジェームス・M・バーダマン 著　　192ページ　ISBN 4-7700-2708-7

日本人英語には共通の「アキレス腱」があります。アメリカ人の筆者が、身近でもっとも頻繁に見聞きする、日本人英語の間違い・勘違いを約150例、一挙にまとめて解説しました。間違いを指摘し、背景を解説するだけでなく、実践的な例文・関連表現も盛り込みましたので、日本人共通の弱点を克服できます。

これを英語で言えますか？

学校で教えてくれない身近な英単語

四捨五入する	round off
5^2	five squared
モーニングコール	wake-up call
ホチキス	stapler
改札口	ticket gate
昇進	promotion
協調介入	coordinated intervention
貸し渋り	credit crunch
介護保険	nursing care insurance
花粉症	hay fever
朝飯前だよ	That's a piece of cake!

講談社インターナショナル 編
232ページ
ISBN 4-7700-2132-1

日本人英語の盲点になっている英単語に、78のジャンルから迫ります。読んでみれば、「なーんだ、こんなやさしい単語だったのか」、「そうか、こう言えば良かったのか」と思いあたる単語や表現がいっぱいです。雑学も満載しましたので、忘れていた単語が生き返ってくるだけでなく、覚えたことが記憶に残ります。弱点克服のボキャビルに最適です。